# Birthday Memory Book

## A lifetime memory book to record birthday celebrations every year

Page designer: Leda Vaneva

Spirala Publishing

Spirala Memories Journals

Copyright © 2014 by Spirala Publishing

All rights reserved. No part of this publication may be reproduced, distributed or transmitted in any form or by any means, including photocopying, recording, or other electronic or mechanical methods, without the prior written permission of the publisher, except in the case of brief quotations embodied in critical reviews and certain other noncommercial uses permitted by copyright law. For permission requests, write to the publisher, addressed "Attention: Permissions Coordinator," at the address below.

## Spirala Publishing

Spirala Publishing
contact@spiralaPublishing.com
www.spiralaPublishing.com

**Publisher's Note**: This is a work of fiction. Names, characters, places, and incidents are a product of the author's imagination. Locales and public names are sometimes used for atmospheric purposes. Any resemblance to actual people, living or dead, or to businesses, companies, events, institutions, or locales is completely coincidental.

Ordering Information:
Quantity sales. Special discounts are available on quantity purchases by corporations, associations, and others. For details, contact the "Special Sales Department" at the address above.

Spirala Journals / My quick family cookbook: A blank recipe book for your favorite recipes - 1st ed.

**Distributed by:**
Speedy Publishing LLC
40 E. Main St. #1156
Newark, DE 19711
www.speedypublishing.co

# *Introduction*

Greetings from all of us at Spirala Publishing! We would like to congratulate you on your interest in the Spirala Memories Journals collection for chronicling your life's precious memories.

Spirala Memories Journals is a specially-crafted series of journals, designed to accompany your family through life's memories. The object of each journal is to help the owner record the special events and occasions through the years, serving as a memory book to help you keep your fondest memories close to your heart.

Special events and occasions and their record as memories is what strengthens family bonds. These memories form a lasting impression that can be cherished, as well as helping one feel the warmth of home. Hence, keeping memories alive by recording them in a memory journal can be a great holiday gift and a treasured tradition for you and the people close to you. Your children will appreciate these memories for years to come.

Recorded memories can serve as a keepsake for your children or anyone you've given these journals as a gift. Keeping memory journals is something that your children can teach their future children about when they are grown, as a part of your family tradition. The journals can also be something that you can share with other special people in your life.

These days, we are so bombarded with information and are so busy with everyday life, that it can be easy to forget just how special quality time and holidays spent with loved ones truly are. Days and events can just blur together and get lost in time. We at Spirala Publishing understand that people like you love these special memories and need some help in keeping a record of them. And so the Spirala Memories Journals collection was born.

Spirala Memories Journals were created with you in mind. Each journal page is designed to be aesthetically pleasing and easy to use.

Each memory book is dedicated to one celebration or holiday. Each book has a page to write your memories and another page to paste a photo of that occasion.

As these journals give another meaning to events that occur during the years by making them extra notable, you can make writing in these journals a special family tradition, effectively establishing the foundations of new family traditions which your children and their children will love.

Imagine having a memory book that you can show to you grandchildren: one that will keep your family stories alive and allow you to easily hand them down to future generations. This is a great gift for your children, and one that will stay with them forever, letting them feel the warmth of home wherever they are in the future.

Would you love to have a record of loving memories that you can look at and share with people who are dear to you? Then start keeping journals that preserve and highlight your memories at their very best. Start with yourself so you can share your beautiful memories later. After all, memories become more special when you show how much you value them.

ENJOY!

Date _____

Age:

Theme of Birthday:

How We Celebrated:

Special Meal:

Funny Moments:

Family & Friends Who Shared This Day:

What I Want to Remember Most:

Accomplishments Made This Year:

Comments:

Place for
your photo

Date _____

Age:

Theme of Birthday:

How We Celebrated:

Special Meal:

Funny Moments:

Family & Friends Who Shared This Day:

What I Want to Remember Most:

Accomplishments Made This Year:

Comments:

Place for
your photo

Date _____

Age:

Theme of Birthday:

How We Celebrated:

Special Meal:

Funny Moments:

Family & Friends Who Shared This Day:

What I Want to Remember Most:

Accomplishments Made This Year:

Comments:

Place for
your photo

Date: _____

Age:

Theme of Birthday:

How We Celebrated:

Special Meal:

Funny Moments:

Family & Friends Who Shared This Day:

What I Want to Remember Most:

Accomplishments Made This Year:

Comments:

Place for
your photo

Date: _____

Age:

Theme of Birthday:

How We Celebrated:

Special Meal:

Funny Moments:

Family & Friends Who Shared This Day:

What I Want to Remember Most:

Accomplishments Made This Year:

Comments:

Place for
your photo

Date _____

Age:

Theme of Birthday:

How We Celebrated:

Special Meal:

Funny Moments:

Family & Friends Who Shared This Day:

What I Want to Remember Most:

Accomplishments Made This Year:

Comments:

Place for
your photo

Date _____

Age:
_____

Theme of Birthday:
_____
_____

How We Celebrated:
_____
_____

Special Meal:
_____
_____

Funny Moments:
_____
_____

Family & Friends Who Shared This Day:
_____
_____

What I Want to Remember Most:
_____
_____

Accomplishments Made This Year:
_____
_____

Comments:

Place for
your photo

Date _____

Age: _____

Theme of Birthday: _____

How We Celebrated: _____

Special Meal: _____

Funny Moments: _____

Family & Friends Who Shared This Day: _____

What I Want to Remember Most: _____

Accomplishments Made This Year: _____

Comments: _____

Place for
your photo

Date _____

Age: _____

Theme of Birthday: _____

How We Celebrated: _____

Special Meal: _____

Funny Moments: _____

Family & Friends Who Shared This Day: _____

What I Want to Remember Most: _____

Accomplishments Made This Year: _____

Comments: _____

Place for
your photo

Date: _____

Age: _____

Theme of Birthday: _____

How We Celebrated: _____

Special Meal: _____

Funny Moments: _____

Family & Friends Who Shared This Day: _____

What I Want to Remember Most: _____

Accomplishments Made This Year: _____

Comments:

Place for
your photo

Date: _____

Age:

Theme of Birthday:

How We Celebrated:

Special Meal:

Funny Moments:

Family & Friends Who Shared This Day:

What I Want to Remember Most:

Accomplishments Made This Year:

Comments:

Place for
your photo

Date _____

Age:

Theme of Birthday:

How We Celebrated:

Special Meal:

Funny Moments:

Family & Friends Who Shared This Day:

What I Want to Remember Most:

Accomplishments Made This Year:

Comments:

Place for
your photo

Date: _____

Age:

Theme of Birthday:

How We Celebrated:

Special Meal:

Funny Moments:

Family & Friends Who Shared This Day:

What I Want to Remember Most:

Accomplishments Made This Year:

Comments:

Place for your photo

Date: _____

Age:

Theme of Birthday:

How We Celebrated:

Special Meal:

Funny Moments:

Family & Friends Who Shared This Day:

What I Want to Remember Most:

Accomplishments Made This Year:

Comments:

Place for
your photo

Date _____

Age: _____

Theme of Birthday: _____
_____

How We Celebrated: _____
_____

Special Meal: _____
_____

Funny Moments: _____
_____

Family & Friends Who Shared This Day: _____
_____

What I Want to Remember Most: _____
_____

Accomplishments Made This Year: _____
_____

Comments:

Place for
your photo

Date _____

Age:

Theme of Birthday:

How We Celebrated:

Special Meal:

Funny Moments:

Family & Friends Who Shared This Day:

What I Want to Remember Most:

Accomplishments Made This Year:

Comments:

Place for
your photo

Date _____

Age: _____

Theme of Birthday: _____

How We Celebrated: _____

Special Meal: _____

Funny Moments: _____

Family & Friends Who Shared This Day: _____

What I Want to Remember Most: _____

Accomplishments Made This Year: _____

Comments: _____

Place for
your photo

Date _____

Age:
_____

Theme of Birthday:
_____

How We Celebrated:
_____
_____

Special Meal:
_____
_____

Funny Moments:
_____
_____

Family & Friends Who Shared This Day:
_____
_____

What I Want to Remember Most:
_____
_____

Accomplishments Made This Year:
_____
_____

Comments:

Place for
your photo

Date _____

Age:

Theme of Birthday:

How We Celebrated:

Special Meal:

Funny Moments:

Family & Friends Who Shared This Day:

What I Want to Remember Most:

Accomplishments Made This Year:

Comments:

Place for
your photo

Date _____

Age: _____

Theme of Birthday: _____

How We Celebrated: _____

Special Meal: _____

Funny Moments: _____

Family & Friends Who Shared This Day: _____

What I Want to Remember Most: _____

Accomplishments Made This Year: _____

Comments: _____

Place for
your photo

Date: _____

Age: _____

Theme of Birthday: _____
_____

How We Celebrated: _____
_____

Special Meal: _____
_____

Funny Moments: _____
_____

Family & Friends Who Shared This Day: _____
_____

What I Want to Remember Most: _____
_____

Accomplishments Made This Year: _____
_____

Comments: _____

Place for
your photo

Date _____

Age:

Theme of Birthday:

How We Celebrated:

Special Meal:

Funny Moments:

Family & Friends Who Shared This Day:

What I Want to Remember Most:

Accomplishments Made This Year:

Comments:

Place for
your photo

Date _____

Age: _____

Theme of Birthday: _____

How We Celebrated: _____

Special Meal: _____

Funny Moments: _____

Family & Friends Who Shared This Day: _____

What I Want to Remember Most: _____

Accomplishments Made This Year: _____

Comments:

Place for
your photo

Date _____

Age:

Theme of Birthday:

How We Celebrated:

Special Meal:

Funny Moments:

Family & Friends Who Shared This Day:

What I Want to Remember Most:

Accomplishments Made This Year:

Comments:

Place for
your photo

Date _____

Age: _____

Theme of Birthday: _____

_____

How We Celebrated: _____

_____

Special Meal: _____

_____

Funny Moments: _____

_____

Family & Friends Who Shared This Day: _____

_____

What I Want to Remember Most: _____

_____

Accomplishments Made This Year: _____

_____

Comments: _____

Place for
your photo

Date _____

Age: _____

Theme of Birthday: _____

_____

How We Celebrated: _____

_____

Special Meal: _____

_____

Funny Moments: _____

_____

Family & Friends Who Shared This Day: _____

_____

What I Want to Remember Most: _____

_____

Accomplishments Made This Year: _____

_____

Comments:

Place for
your photo

Date: _____

Age: _____

Theme of Birthday: _____

How We Celebrated: _____

Special Meal: _____

Funny Moments: _____

Family & Friends Who Shared This Day: _____

What I Want to Remember Most: _____

Accomplishments Made This Year: _____

Comments: _____

Place for
your photo

Date _____

Age: _____

Theme of Birthday:

_____

How We Celebrated:

_____

Special Meal:

_____

Funny Moments:

_____

Family & Friends Who Shared This Day:

_____

What I Want to Remember Most:

_____

Accomplishments Made This Year:

_____

Comments:

Place for
your photo

Date _____

Age:

Theme of Birthday:

How We Celebrated:

Special Meal:

Funny Moments:

Family & Friends Who Shared This Day:

What I Want to Remember Most:

Accomplishments Made This Year:

Comments:

Place for
your photo

Date: _____

Age:

Theme of Birthday:

How We Celebrated:

Special Meal:

Funny Moments:

Family & Friends Who Shared This Day:

What I Want to Remember Most:

Accomplishments Made This Year:

Comments:

Place for
your photo

Date: _____

Age:

Theme of Birthday:

How We Celebrated:

Special Meal:

Funny Moments:

Family & Friends Who Shared This Day:

What I Want to Remember Most:

Accomplishments Made This Year:

Comments:

Place for
your photo

Date: _____

Age: _____

Theme of Birthday: _____

_____

How We Celebrated: _____

_____

Special Meal: _____

_____

Funny Moments: _____

_____

Family & Friends Who Shared This Day: _____

_____

What I Want to Remember Most: _____

_____

Accomplishments Made This Year: _____

_____

Comments: _____

Place for your photo

Date _____

Age:

Theme of Birthday:

How We Celebrated:

Special Meal:

Funny Moments:

Family & Friends Who Shared This Day:

What I Want to Remember Most:

Accomplishments Made This Year:

Comments:

Place for
your photo

Date: _____

Age: _____

Theme of Birthday: _____

How We Celebrated: _____

Special Meal: _____

Funny Moments: _____

Family & Friends Who Shared This Day: _____

What I Want to Remember Most: _____

Accomplishments Made This Year: _____

Comments:

Place for
your photo

Date _____

Age: _____

Theme of Birthday: _____

_____

How We Celebrated: _____

_____

Special Meal: _____

_____

Funny Moments: _____

_____

Family & Friends Who Shared This Day: _____

_____

What I Want to Remember Most: _____

_____

Accomplishments Made This Year: _____

_____

Comments: _____

Place for
your photo

Date _____

Age: _____

Theme of Birthday: _____

How We Celebrated: _____

Special Meal: _____

Funny Moments: _____

Family & Friends Who Shared This Day: _____

What I Want to Remember Most: _____

Accomplishments Made This Year: _____

Comments:

Place for
your photo

Date _____

Age: _____

Theme of Birthday: _____
_____

How We Celebrated: _____
_____

Special Meal: _____
_____

Funny Moments: _____
_____

Family & Friends Who Shared This Day: _____
_____

What I Want to Remember Most: _____
_____

Accomplishments Made This Year: _____
_____

Comments:

Place for
your photo

Date _____

Age:

Theme of Birthday:

How We Celebrated:

Special Meal:

Funny Moments:

Family & Friends Who Shared This Day:

What I Want to Remember Most:

Accomplishments Made This Year:

Comments:

Place for your photo

Date _____

Age: _____

Theme of Birthday: _____

_____

How We Celebrated: _____

_____

Special Meal: _____

_____

Funny Moments: _____

_____

Family & Friends Who Shared This Day: ___

_____

What I Want to Remember Most: _____

_____

Accomplishments Made This Year: _____

_____

Comments:

Date _____

Age: _____

Theme of Birthday: _____

_____

How We Celebrated: _____

_____

Special Meal: _____

_____

Funny Moments: _____

_____

Family & Friends Who Shared This Day: _____

_____

What I Want to Remember Most: _____

_____

Accomplishments Made This Year: _____

_____

Comments: _____

Place for
your photo

Date: _____

Age: _____

Theme of Birthday: _____

How We Celebrated: _____

Special Meal: _____

Funny Moments: _____

Family & Friends Who Shared This Day: _____

What I Want to Remember Most: _____

Accomplishments Made This Year: _____

Comments: _____

Place for
your photo

Date: _____

Age:
_____

Theme of Birthday:
_____

How We Celebrated:
_____

Special Meal:
_____

Funny Moments:
_____

Family & Friends Who Shared This Day:
_____

What I Want to Remember Most:
_____

Accomplishments Made This Year:
_____

Comments:

Place for your photo

Date _____

Age: _____

Theme of Birthday: _____

How We Celebrated: _____

Special Meal: _____

Funny Moments: _____

Family & Friends Who Shared This Day: _____

What I Want to Remember Most: _____

Accomplishments Made This Year: _____

Comments: _____

Date _____

Age:

Theme of Birthday:

How We Celebrated:

Special Meal:

Funny Moments:

Family & Friends Who Shared This Day:

What I Want to Remember Most:

Accomplishments Made This Year:

Comments:

Place for your photo

Date: _____

Age:

Theme of Birthday:

How We Celebrated:

Special Meal:

Funny Moments:

Family & Friends Who Shared This Day:

What I Want to Remember Most:

Accomplishments Made This Year:

Comments:

Date _____

Age: _____

Theme of Birthday:

_____

How We Celebrated:

_____

Special Meal:

_____

Funny Moments:

_____

Family & Friends Who Shared This Day:

_____

What I Want to Remember Most:

_____

Accomplishments Made This Year:

_____

Comments:

Place for
your photo

Date _____

Age: _____

Theme of Birthday: _____

How We Celebrated: _____

Special Meal: _____

Funny Moments: _____

Family & Friends Who Shared This Day: _____

What I Want to Remember Most: _____

Accomplishments Made This Year: _____

Comments: _____

Place for
your photo

Date _____

Age: _____

Theme of Birthday: _____

_____

How We Celebrated: _____

_____

Special Meal: _____

_____

Funny Moments: _____

_____

Family & Friends Who Shared This Day: _____

_____

What I Want to Remember Most: _____

_____

Accomplishments Made This Year: _____

_____

Comments:

Place for
your photo

Date _____

Age: _____

Theme of Birthday: _____

How We Celebrated: _____

Special Meal: _____

Funny Moments: _____

Family & Friends Who Shared This Day: _____

What I Want to Remember Most: _____

Accomplishments Made This Year: _____

Comments:

Place for
your photo

Date _____

Age: _____

Theme of Birthday:
_____

How We Celebrated:
_____

Special Meal:
_____

Funny Moments:
_____

Family & Friends Who Shared This Day:
_____

What I Want to Remember Most:
_____

Accomplishments Made This Year:
_____

Comments:

Place for your photo

# Spirala Memories Journals Collection

Visit our website to purchase more journals from this collection.

www.SpiralaPublishing.com/SpiralaMemories

# Spirala Publishing

**Cutting Edge Products with Quality Built In**

Visit our website to see our full collection of books, journals, memory books, coloring books and more.

### www.SpiralaPublishing.com

Enjoy a variety of our famous and well-known product lines, such as:

- *Learn & Color* Coloring Book series
- *Holidays & Celebrations* Coloring Book series
- *Spirala Journals*
- *Spirala Memories Journals*
- *My Pregnancy Toolkit*

**Cutting Edge Products with Quality Built In**

Be the first to know about new products and other events. Sign up to receive the Spirala Publishing Newsletter via your E-mail address.

### www.SpiralaPublishing.com/signup